A CHRISTMAS TRAIN ACROSS CANADA

A CHRISTMAS TRAIN ACROSS CANADA

Christmas Around the World
From World Book

World Book, Inc.
a Scott Fetzer company
Chicago
www.worldbook.com

STAFF

World Book, Inc.
233 North Michigan Avenue
Chicago, Illinois 60601 U.S.A.

Library of Congress Cataloging-in-Publication Data

A Christmas train across Canada.
    pages cm. -- (Christmas around the world from World Book)
    Summary: "A trip across Canada at Christmas time by train, including information on Canadian Christmas customs; provides in-depth information on Winter and Christmas events in Vancouver, the Canadian Rockies and Banff, Calgary, Toronto, Montreal, Quebec City, and Cape Breton. Also includes crafts, recipes, and carols"-- Provided by publisher.
    ISBN 978-0-7166-0828-8
    1. Christmas--Canada--Juvenile literature. 2. Canada--Social life and customs--Juvenile literature. I. World Book, Inc.
GT4987.15.C49 2014
394.26630971--dc23
                    2014024078

Printed in China by Shenzhen Donnelley Printing Co., Ltd., Guangdong Province
1st printing September 2014

Note: This book features an imaginative train trip. Schedules between cities and regions in this book may not be accurate for planning purposes. Please see a travel agent or the Internet to book your Canadian train trip.

"D'où Viens-Tu, Bergère? (Whence Art Thou, My Maiden?)" and "'Twas in the Moon of Wintertime" from the *International Book of Christmas Carols,* copyright © 1963, 1980 by Walter Ehret and George K. Evans. © Walton Music Corp. Used by permission.

CONTENTS

A TRAIN ACROSS CANADA

Since 1885, the year that the final spike was hammered into Canada's first transcontinental railroad, people have marveled at the beauty to be seen by rail in Canada. From the coastal city of Vancouver, British Columbia; through the Canadian Rockies; and on to Toronto, Quebec City, and Halifax, Canada is home to breathtaking natural beauty. The charm of train travel, with the sights from the observation car, the convivial atmosphere of the club car, and the dining car—a sit-down restaurant on wheels—adds so much to the experience.

While Canada is beautiful all year, it is especially lovely at Christmastime. Canada's winter scenery is picture-postcard pretty, with huge stands of snowy pines, clear and cold lakes, and the majestic Canadian Rockies.

To travel through this scenery by train is a dream come true.

AT CHRISTMASTIME

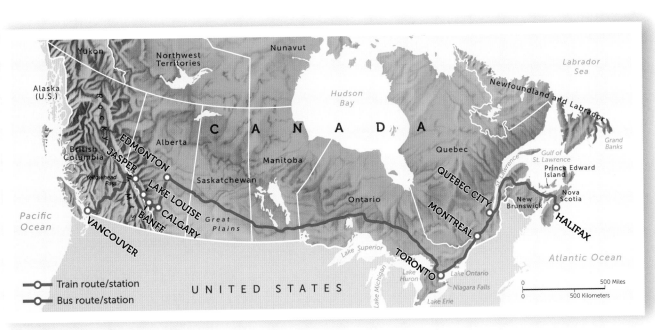

British Customs

The British were the first Europeans to formally stake a claim in land that is now Canada, making the claim for England in 1497 when explorer John Cabot declared the land for Henry VII (1457-1509). Although immigrants from many nations have since come to Canada, British traditions and customs still form an important part of Canadian culture. Today, about one-third of Canadians have some British ancestry, and never is the British influence in Canada more apparent than at Christmastime.

Canadian customs brought from England by early British settlers

Early British settlers had to make many adaptations to the Christmas customs they followed because Canada's plants, animals, and climate were very different from their native England. Instead of English holly and mistletoe, the British settlers collected wintergreen, hemlock, cedar, and spruce from the woods around them. They twisted evergreen boughs into garlands to drape over mantels and tuck above pictures. They added native high-bush cranberries, mountain ash, or strings of coral beads to the greenery for a splash of color. A fortunate family might set out a centerpiece bowl of fruits and nuts or add colorful ribbons and white tallow candles to their greenery here and there. In Anglican churches, sprigs of cedar might be tucked into drilled holes in the pews. Seasonal greenery decorated the altar, and festive banners were often hung on the walls.

Early settlers made kissing boughs. Hung in a hallway or doorway, the kissing bough—also called a kissing ball—consisted of a globe or ring made of evergreen boughs and decorated with candles, apples, and nuts (one appears in the print at right). The British custom of a kissing bough dates back to at least medieval times; it is a pre-Christian symbol of the return of light and life to the world following the winter solstice. The custom has always been popular, as the bough earned its name by granting a free kiss to couples caught under its spell.

Customs brought from Britain during the Victorian era

Before the mid-1800's, there were no Christmas trees in British homes. According to tradition, German-born Prince Albert, the husband of British Queen Victoria (reigned from 1837-1901), introduced the German custom of the Christmas tree to England. In actuality, an earlier royal, German-born Charlotte, wife of George III

(reigned from 1760-1820), introduced the Christmas tree to the British. During Charlotte's reign, the German custom was to celebrate Christmas with a yew bough, a tree branch that was decorated and lighted with candles. In England, Charlotte celebrated Christmas with a yew branch in the late 1700's. In 1800, however, she had an entire tree brought into Queen's Lodge, Windsor Castle, and had it lighted and decorated—England's first Christmas tree.

Though Prince Albert may not have introduced the Christmas tree to the British court, he was the one who introduced it to the British public, who were intensely interested in young Victoria's German-born husband. Engravings and stories about the royal couple and their children were common in newspapers of the day, including stories of how they celebrated Christmas at Windsor Castle. Images of a Christmas tree at the castle inspired the

Advent begins on the fourth Sunday before Christmas and ends on Christmas Eve. The British Christmas season begins on the last Sunday before Advent, called "Stir-Up Sunday." It is named for the collect (KOL ehkt) from the Anglican *Book of Common Prayer* read on this day, which begins "Stir up, we beseech thee, O Lord, the wills of thy faithful people. ..." As shown in this print from 1881 of a Stir-Up Sunday, the family assembles in the kitchen to mix the pudding, and each member makes a wish. Then the pudding is covered and stored until Christmas Day.

A print from an 1848 *Illustrated London News* shows Queen Victoria and Prince Albert celebrating with family around the Christmas tree. This image is, at least in part, credited with sparking the popularity of the custom of a decorated tree in the home.

upper classes to adopt the tradition of a tree. Eventually, the custom spread to the British middle class and to other nations that celebrated Christmas, such as Canada and the United States.

The popular Christmas tree is not the only custom that the Victorians (as the people who lived during the reign of Queen Victoria are known) made popular.

The focus on children at Christmas also dates to Victorian times. In the mid- to late-1800's, people developed a new interest in children and their unique needs—creating a new emphasis on toys, play, and books written especially for children. This focus translated to Christmas as well in Victorian England. For example, Father Christmas dates to medieval times. But, before the Victorians, he was portrayed as an old man who joined in with adults in feasting and drinking at Christmas. By the 1870's, he had become an old man who delivered presents to children, and customs surrounding him had been merged with those of the Dutch St. Nicholas.

One final impetus for changes in how Victorians celebrated Christmas was the work of Charles Dickens (1812-1870). This immensely popular British novelist changed the meaning of Christmas for the British, and for much of the English-speaking world. In some part, because of attitudes held by the Puritans about Christmas, the holiday was nearly a dying tradition in the United Kingdom when Dickens began his one-man mission to revive, and sometimes really to invent, Christmas customs.

Some of the changes we see that most likely came to us from Dickens's writings on Christmas include Christmas celebrations being centered on the family. Earlier Christmas feasts were more of a community affair involving the entire village. Dickens's vision of Christmas changed that. From then on, the feasting would be among close family members. Also, in traditional celebrations of the past, Christmas was celebrated for 12 days, from December 25

A hand-colored lithograph from 1840 illustrates a family's pursuits at Christmastime, including singing, dancing, and such games as blind-man's buff. The center image features the family at Christmas dinner with a large pudding.

Twelfth Night

An engraving by artist Joseph Nash (1809-1878) depicts a Twelfth Night celebration in England. Canadians of British descent customarily closed the Christmas season with a dinner party and special cake on Twelfth Night (January 6, the feast date of the Epiphany). The celebration was similar to that celebrated by French Catholics. Finding a bean and a pea baked into the Twelfth Night Cake determined a "king" and "queen" to rule over the night's festivities.

until the Feast of the Epiphany, or Twelfth Night, on January 6. Dickens's writings instituted the change of celebrating heartily, but just for Christmas Eve and Christmas Day. Other ideas fostered by Dickens include Christmas as a time to be generous to the poor; as a time of nostalgia and of looking back to the traditions of earlier times; and as a time to sing Christmas carols and for parents to give children gifts.

As the culture of Christmas changed for the British in the United Kingdom, it began changing for people in former colonies as well. In areas of Canada under British influence, nearly all of the Christmas customs instituted by the Victorians were adopted by Canadians.

An English Christmas, but a Scottish New Year

For Canadian settlers from Scotland, Christmas Day was an occasion for pious religious observance, but not a day of celebration. Some early Scottish immigrants even considered it a working day until Christmas was declared an official holiday in Canada in 1867.

Scottish settlers didn't mind working while others feasted on Christmas Day. They knew that their day of celebration was close at hand. Hogmanay (HOG muh NAY) is the grand Scottish New Year's Eve celebration that begins at midnight.

Hogmanay came into being when Christmas festivities were banned at the time of the Protestant Reformation (from around 1517 to 1648). Today, while it may have faded elsewhere, Hogmanay lives on with vigor in Scotland and among Canadians of Scottish descent. Because the New Year is a time of new beginnings, a Scottish household prepares for this special night with a thorough cleaning.

Bedding is changed, clothes mended, instruments tuned, and brass polished. Each person also sets out to repay any debts and to return anything borrowed. Everyone wants to begin the new year with a clean slate.

A Hogmanay party on New Year's Eve is full of fun and dancing. Friends and family are invited to enjoy a delicious assortment of food. At one point, such a party would have included superstitions and customs. For example, at the stroke of midnight, doors and windows all over the house were thrown open, pots and pans banged, bells rung, and noisemakers rattled to drive out the evil spirits and bad luck of the old year. Then all was shut up tight to allow good to flourish in the New Year.

Not all of these customs are still followed in Scotland, or by people of Scots ancestry, but the custom of the "first-footer," the first person to enter the house after midnight, is still thought to determine the luck of the house in the year ahead. Good luck comes when a dark-haired man is the first-footer. And, at one time at least, all visitors to a house at New Year's, and particularly the first-footer, would carry in bread, salt, and coal, which symbolized life, hospitality, and warmth for the household in the year to come.

All Aboard—
VANCOUVER

We start our tour of Canada at Christmastime in Canada's beautiful city of Vancouver. Located in British Columbia, about 25 miles (40 kilometers) north of the Canadian-United States border, Vancouver is the province's major center of commerce, culture, industry, and transportation. The city has a natural harbor—connected with the Pacific Ocean—that can be used the year around because the harbor's waters never freeze.

People of British ancestry make up the largest ethnic group in Vancouver, so many of the customs of the city are British in origin. But, of course, customs are also tailored to Vancouver's beautiful climate and setting.

The skyline of downtown Vancouver—seen across False Creek with the mountains in the distance—is an exhilarating sight.

Bright Lights CITY NIGHTS

Vancouver's Festival of Lights (above) is held every December in the VanDusen Botanical Garden. A light show is held at the main pond every 30 minutes. All of the grounds are also lighted up to encourage visitors to ramble.

For Bright Nights in Stanley Park (right), millions of Christmas lights are annually installed in the park. Visitors to Bright Nights can also ride a miniature train around the park and visit Santa.

The ice-skating rink (above) in Robson Square decorated for
Christmas: The rink's glass roof is covered in snow. Robson Square
is a public plaza built below street level in downtown Vancouver.
The square underwent a major renovation in 2009, just before the
2010 Winter Olympics hosted by Vancouver.

Capilano Suspension Bridge Park

At Christmastime, Capilano Suspension Bridge Park holds Canyon Lights, with hundreds of thousands of lights decorating the park's temperate rain forest. The original suspension bridge in the park, which crosses the Capilano River, was built in 1889. The modern bridge stretches 450 feet (137 meters) across and 230 feet (70 meters) above the Capilano River.

Tea Time & MORE

The Hotel Vancouver (right) is a landmark in the city. Afternoon tea (inset) at the hotel is a holiday tradition. The restaurant where tea is served—on the hotel's 15th floor, under the soaring copper roof—offers unparalleled views.

The city's Christmas Market, held in Queen Elizabeth Plaza, is a German market where ornaments, handmade toys, and many other items are sold. Christmas food and drink, such as *Lebkuchen* (German cookies) and *Stollen* (Christmas coffee cake) are also available.

The first transcontinental train reached Vancouver from eastern Canada in 1887. We begin our train journey across Canada from one of the nation's earliest transcontinental destinations. The Pacific Central Station (above) opened in 1919.

THE ROCKY MOUNTAINS—
Jasper, Lake Louise, and Banff

In Jasper National Park, mountains are reflected in the water of the Athabasca River.

We are using a tour service between Vancouver and Calgary. During winter, there is no train service in the heart of the Canadian Rockies, so we will be bused between locations in that area. We begin our journey east in the evening on *The Canadian*. We ride overnight in a sleeper car as the train passes some of British Columbia's dry and desertlike interior. By lunchtime of the next day, we are surrounded by the scenic beauty of the Rockies. We travel through Yellowhead Pass, an opening through the Continental Divide of the Americas. (*Continental Divide* is the term used to designate the line of elevated land that separates areas drained to opposite sides of a continent.)

Some of the sights to be seen on this journey include Pyramid Falls. (This waterfall, which makes a 300-foot [90-meter] drop in summer, is frozen solid in winter.) Other beautiful sights are the Albreda Icefields Glacier, Mount Robson, Moose Lake, and the Fraser River. By late afternoon we enter Jasper National Park in the Athabasca River valley in Alberta.

Jasper has a great number of winter activities; in addition to skiing and snowboarding in Marmot Basin, there are Nordic trails for cross-country skiing. Stargazing should also be on your list of things to do, as Jasper National Park is one of the world's largest dark-sky preserves. A guided hike in Maligne Canyon, a deep limestone gorge riddled with caves, can be taken at night. The frozen waterfalls in the canyon look magical.

After a day in Jasper, we take a bus along the Icefield Parkways, one of the world's most scenic roads. Lake Louise is a short distance from Jasper, only about 145 miles (233 kilometers) south. On the way to Lake Louise, we pass the Athabasca Glacier. This huge glacier is 3 miles (6 kilometers) long and 0.6 mile (1 kilometer) wide. Part of the Columbia Icefields, this is one of only a few places in the world that forms a triple continental divide. The water here flows north to the Arctic Ocean, east to the Atlantic, and west to the Pacific. (Other triple divides are in Glacier National Park in the U.S. state of Montana and in Siberia in Russia.)

Lake Louise

We arrive at the charming village of Lake Louise to stay at the Chateau Lake Louise in Banff National Park. This hotel (below) and the luxury hotel near the town of Banff, the Banff Springs, were founded by Cornelius Van Horne, the general manager of the Canadian Pacific Railway in the late 1800's. Van Horne wanted to create destinations that would encourage people to use his railway. He encouraged the Canadian Pacific Railway to build a string of luxury hotels across Canada to drum up tourism.

Ice sculptures are a feature of Chateau Lake Louise in winter (left). Other Christmas activities at the hotel include caroling and sipping hot chocolate while looking out over a beautiful view of the lake and mountains.

Lake Louise offers a number of snowshoeing tours. Snowshoeing is essentially walking, so nearly anyone who can walk can do it.

Sleigh rides along the shore of frozen Lake Louise afford scenic views to passengers.

Banff

After two nights and a day in Lake Louise, we leave by bus for Banff. Banff is a small town catering to tourists and skiers in Banff National Park, which was founded in 1887 under the name Rocky Mountain National Park. It was Canada's first national park and the third such park to open in the world at the time.

One of the great treats during our tour of the Rockies will be our hotel in Banff—the Banff Springs Hotel (above and below), sometimes called the "Castle in the Rockies."

In addition to skiing and snowboarding, Banff has other outdoor attractions. The hot springs at Banff (above) are world famous, featuring natural mineral water kept at temperatures between 98 and 104 °F (37 and 40 °C). The site has a historic bathhouse; people have been coming to Banff to take the waters for more than 100 years.

Try a tour by dog sled. Let enthusiastic and energetic Alaskan huskies (and their musher) show you the beauty of Banff National Park.

Next stop—
CALGARY

We leave Banff and travel by bus to Calgary, the largest city in the province of Alberta. Nearly half the people in Calgary have some British ancestry. Calgary began as a cattle town and is still a major cattle center in Alberta. The city has won fame for the yearly Calgary Stampede in July, which features chuck wagon races, livestock shows, rodeo events, and carnival rides and games. Today, Calgary is the oil center of Canada.

Calgary in winter can have unpredictable weather. Because the city is close to the Rockies, warming winds called chinooks sweep over Calgary, causing it to be the warmest of the prairie cities. Nevertheless, Calgary can also suddenly receive a foot (0.3 meter) of snow.

Calgary is a big city whose people have retained their small-town charm.

Day and **NIGHT**

Calgary's Heritage Park
Historical Village, Canada's
largest living history
museum, hosts Christmas
events: snow painting
(creating images in snow
using food coloring and
water); decorating ginger-
bread cookies; or talking
with Santa.

Heritage Park Historical
Village offers horse-drawn
wagon rides.

Christmas events in Calgary include Zoolights, held by the Calgary Zoo. Much of the zoo is located on St. George's Island, surrounded by the Bow River. The Calgary Zoo decorates with more than 1.5 million lights at Christmastime. There is also an area where kids can build their own igloo. Visitors can warm up with an outdoor fire and a cup of cocoa.

THE GREAT PLAINS

We catch the Red Arrow bus in Calgary and travel to Edmonton. In Edmonton, we board *The Canadian* to travel across Canada's Great Plains to Toronto, a distance of more than 2,000 miles (3,200 kilometers). The Great Plains is a vast, dry grassland in North America that stretches from Canada to Mexico. The plains were first inhabited by Indians, but the railroads that were built to the west in the 1800's led to the plains being populated by Europeans with towns, ranches, and farms. Crossing in winter gives the impression of huge empty fields for much of the plains, but in reality the region is one of the world's chief wheat-growing areas, and in summer the view is of cereal crops as far as the eye can see.

The northern lights, or aurora borealis, a natural display of light in the sky, shine over Canada's Great Plains in Manitoba.

A bison, sometimes called a buffalo, grazes on the Great Plains of Canada, in Alberta.

Right on time—
TORONTO

Toronto, Ontario's capital and Canada's largest city, lies on the northwest shore of Lake Ontario. The city was founded in 1793 by John Graves Simcoe, lieutenant governor of the British colony of Upper Canada (the southern part of what is now Ontario). Simcoe chose the site of present-day Toronto for a new colonial capital.

Toronto is a large, sophisticated city. We are taking a few days here to see some tourist sights in addition to enjoying Christmas events. Our first tourist outing is a day trip to a spectacular natural wonder, Niagara Falls. The falls are on the Niagara River, about halfway between Lake Erie and Lake Ontario. The river forms part of the United States-Canadian border.

Evening skaters at Nathan Phillips Square, in front of Toronto's city hall.

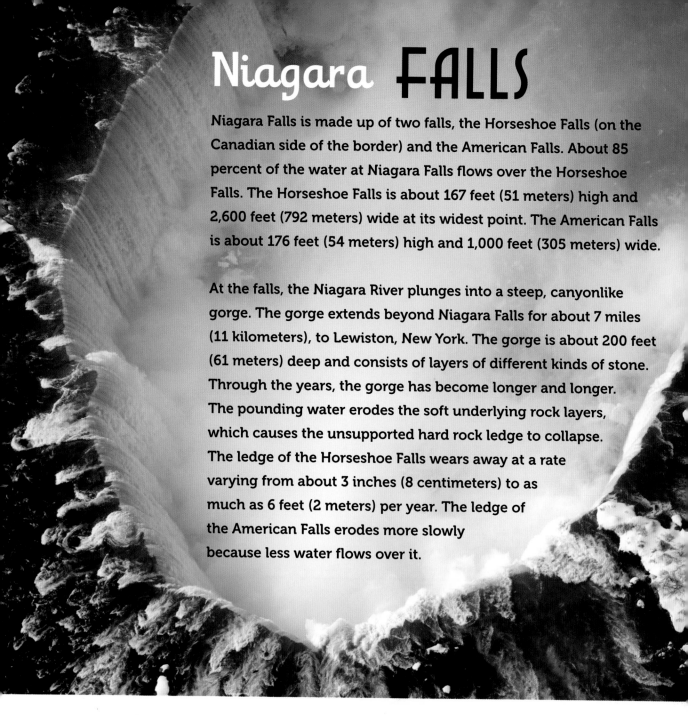

Niagara FALLS

Niagara Falls is made up of two falls, the Horseshoe Falls (on the Canadian side of the border) and the American Falls. About 85 percent of the water at Niagara Falls flows over the Horseshoe Falls. The Horseshoe Falls is about 167 feet (51 meters) high and 2,600 feet (792 meters) wide at its widest point. The American Falls is about 176 feet (54 meters) high and 1,000 feet (305 meters) wide.

At the falls, the Niagara River plunges into a steep, canyonlike gorge. The gorge extends beyond Niagara Falls for about 7 miles (11 kilometers), to Lewiston, New York. The gorge is about 200 feet (61 meters) deep and consists of layers of different kinds of stone. Through the years, the gorge has become longer and longer. The pounding water erodes the soft underlying rock layers, which causes the unsupported hard rock ledge to collapse. The ledge of the Horseshoe Falls wears away at a rate varying from about 3 inches (8 centimeters) to as much as 6 feet (2 meters) per year. The ledge of the American Falls erodes more slowly because less water flows over it.

At Table Rock, we take the Journey Behind the Falls tour. The short walking tour allows visitors to view the falls from behind via observation platforms and tunnels.

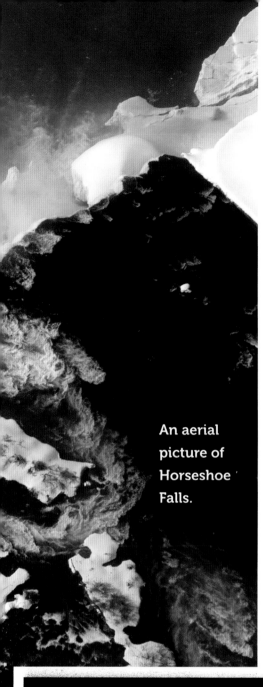

An aerial picture of Horseshoe Falls.

Some attractions at Niagara are not available in winter—for example, boat tours on the *Maid of the Mist* are only possible between Memorial Day and Labor Day. Most things are still open, however. One of the best ways to see the falls is on foot. The walk along the gorge from the Rainbow Bridge to Table Rock is breathtaking.

In the evening, we stop at the town of Niagara Falls, Canada, for their Festival of Lights. A 3-mile (5-kilometer) pathway is decorated with 3 million lights for this winter display. Fireworks displays are also given in the evening.

Time for SHOPPING

A Christmas window (above)
from a Hudson's Bay Company
department store in Toronto.
The company is one of the oldest
North American corporations;
it was formed by charter in 1670
as a fur-trading company.

Christmas shopping under
the glass galleria of Toronto's
Eaton Centre mall.

The next day, we attend Toronto's European Christmas Market in its historic Distillery District. The market features traditional foods, music, folk dance, and a beer garden, along with vendors selling traditional Christmas items—such as ornaments, crèche figures, and hand-carved angels. The Distillery District centers on the restored red brick, Victorian-era buildings of the Gooderham & Worts whiskey distillery. The distillery was closed in 1990 and now holds boutiques, shops, and cafes in its buildings.

We leave the colorful Christmas lights of Toronto and travel by train to historic Montreal and Quebec City. We are traveling not just to a different place, but also to a different culture. Up until now, the places we have visited were settled by the British, and these places still follow British customs at Christmastime. But from the early 1600's to the mid-1700's, the region that is now the province of Quebec was settled by France. A large number of the people who live in Quebec today speak French and follow French customs at Christmas.

French Customs

Viking ships are said to have visited the Atlantic coast of Canada nearly 1,000 years ago. In the summer of 1497, John Cabot touched shore at Newfoundland and claimed the territory for England. Soon after Cabot's discovery, European companies began making annual expeditions to the fertile fishing grounds of the Grand Banks off Newfoundland's coast.

Still, it was the French who took the lead in exploring Canada. French explorer Samuel de Champlain established a permanent settlement, founding the city of Quebec in 1608. French trappers and traders were the first to explore Canada's deep woods. Today, French Canadians—descendants of those early French explorers, trappers, and settlers—comprise a little over 20 percent of Canada's population.

Early Christmas Celebrations

In years past, the religious celebration of Christmas for French Canadians began at the close of November, on the first Sunday of Advent—and so did the work. Weeks of preparation were needed to ready the array of offerings for the sumptuous Christmas feast, the New Year's Day celebration, and the week of parties and hungry visitors in between.

First came the meats—beef, pork, chicken, wild game, partridges, and turkeys—to be readied for pies, stews, and soups. Then, dozens upon dozens of doughnuts were fried, tossed in sugar, stored in freshly laundered pillowcases, and hung in the meat freezer. There they would hang until Christmas Eve.

Preparing the food for Christmas was sometimes more fun than work. In times past, a taffy pull party, held on November 25 in honor of Saint Catherine of Alexandria, the patron saint of single women, was one of the first delights of the Christmas season. Presented as a working session to prepare candy for Christmas, taffy pulls offered a chance for eligible bachelors and single young women from farms all around the area to get to know each other before the rush of Christmas parties.

After weeks of anticipation and preparation, Christmas arrived for French Canadians with *la messe de minuit* (lah mess duh min wee), the midnight Mass on Christmas Eve. Earlier in the evening, young children would hang up their stockings and climb into bed. The older children and other family members would decorate the Christmas tree with

An artist's depiction of French Canadian villagers arriving at church in horse-drawn sleighs on a snowy Christmas Eve in the 1800's.

lights, golden angels, and garlands of silver. They would then place a small manger scene or crèche under the tree. The *crèche* (cresh)—a cherished Christmas tradition today throughout North America—was introduced to Canadians by French settlers.

Soon it would be time for the family to venture off to church. When recalling Christmases past, many French Canadians tell of fond memories of being awakened by their parents, bundled into warm clothes, and carried off into the frigid, starry night to the wonders of this

Mass. The feeling inspired was powerful. Gazing at the church's carved wood warmed by candlelight, the stained-glass windows, and the figures of the life-sized crèche, those attending the service sang beloved carols and listened to the story of the Christ Child's birth. Traditionally, there were three Masses: the first and most solemn, Night Mass; the Dawn Mass; and the Day Mass. These church services extended the religious celebration into the light of Christmas Day.

Réveillon

While it was traditional for the entire extended family to attend midnight Mass together, the people doing the cooking remained home during the service. After all, there was important work to be done: Cakes needed icing, turkeys needed basting, and tables needed last-minute, festive touches. Those who remained behind knew that the moment the last hymn ended, all in attendance at Mass would rush home for *réveillon* (reh vay yon), or "awakening," the family meal that had kept the cooks busy for weeks.

La tourtière (TOHRT yair), a meat pie, was the highlight of *réveillon,* but it always had plenty of company. Other meat dishes included *ragoût de boulettes* (rah goo duh booh let), a meatball and pork hocks stew; minced pork pie; partridge with cabbage; and a goose or turkey. *Les cretons* (lez cray tawn), a traditional Quebec pork spread (similar to pâté) was truly a must. Side dishes included oyster or pea soup, a variety of homemade cheese sauces, homemade ketchups, sweet pickles and relishes, chutney, and cranberry sauce.

To top off this traditional meal, at least four or five desserts were served. A variety of pastries and candies, bread pudding, corn-meal cake, fruitcakes, sugar pie, maple-syrup tarts, and ice cream all had a presence on the dessert table. And one could not forget the doughnuts, fresh from the pillowcases.

Some early French Canadians carried on the European tradition of the Yule log by burning a special birch Christmas log in the fireplace during réveillon. Later, the log was symbolically replaced by the *bûche de Noël* (BOOSH duh noh ehl), a chocolate cake shaped like a log and topped with chocolate icing formed into barklike ridges or a drizzling of white "snow" icing. This special Christmas cake remains a tradition with many Quebec families today.

In the countryside, *réveillon* was usually served in the farm kitchen. However, any room that could accommodate at least two tables and the 20 to 30 family members in attendance would do. Often adding to their celebration was a fiddler who would play for hours, enticing all

An illustration from a children's magazine in the 1920's depicts the start of the *réveillon* feast.

takers to show off their folk-dancing talents. With its many courses, multiple tempting desserts, and plenty of good cheer, the *réveillon* feast often lasted well into the early hours of the morning.

Traditionally, children received presents from their relatives during the *réveillon* celebration. And their stockings often would be filled with oranges, nuts, and little candies from *Père Noël* (pehr noh ehl).

However, the true gift giving by custom was reserved for New Year's Day.

Christmas Day itself was a time of relaxation for the adults and games and outdoor sports for the children. The activities were often followed by a small family dinner in the evening.

New Year's Day

For French Canadians, New Year's Day has always been a time for gathering with family and friends. While réveillon was traditionally a family-only celebration, New Year's Day was the time to throw open the doors and welcome in friends and neighbors alike.

On this, the first day of the year, every child asked for his or her father's blessing. Grown children living far away would return for this important event and the entire family would come together to receive the patriarch's blessing for the year. Following a morning church service, holiday fare filled the tables for visitors who came calling to exchange best wishes for the New Year. By evening, friends and family would join together in singing, dancing, and other entertainment.

New Year's Day was also the day gifts were exchanged, and children received their presents at long last—from the Infant Jesus or Père Noël in alternating years.

Quebec's Christmas Today

When France lost the Quebec region to England in 1763, about 65,000 French colonists resided there. Today, there are approximately six million Canadians in Quebec who speak French as their native language. French is the official language of the province, and Quebec's citizens proudly preserve their uniquely French-Canadian culture.

It is no surprise, then, that French Canadians continue to observe their French Christmas traditions, adding a pinch of modern flavor here and there. Midnight Mass is still the spiritual heart of Christmas, and réveillon is nearly unchanged. Naturally, some families have chosen to add a few "nouvelle cuisine" dishes to their menus.

A family in Montreal may attend midnight Mass at the world-famous St. Joseph's Oratory, which houses a collection of Nativity scenes from around the world. Or they may celebrate the Christ child's birth in Old Montreal at Notre-Dame Basilica. Here, they listen to beloved Christmas hymns and carols played on the 5,772-pipe organ, while taking in the church's monumental altar and exquisite woodcarvings.

Before attending church services on Christmas Eve and Christmas Day, many city dwellers celebrate with sleigh-rides, cross-country skiing, and ice-skating parties in Montreal's Mount Royal Park. Located in the heart of the city, the park offers miles of snowy trails through groves of tall maple and oak trees, its own 769-foot (234-meter) mountain, and picturesque Beaver Lake. There is no more perfect site for outdoor winter fun. Some Quebec City residents make the short trip up the river to *Ste.-Anne-de-Beaupré* (sent ahn duh booh pray) to celebrate Christ's birth in the most-visited basilica in North America. With its striking Gothic and Romanesque architecture and its 240 stained-glass windows, Ste.-Anne's is a beautiful setting in which to celebrate this holy season.

While some French-Canadian families still save gift-giving for New Year's Day, most children look for filled stockings and presents under the tree after réveillon or on Christmas morning. Some lucky French-Canadian children receive presents on Christmas and New Year's Day.

The first day of the New Year continues to be a very special day of celebration for French-Canadian families. It is still customary for children to seek the blessing of the head of the family—their grandfather, father, or oldest brother—as the New Year begins. Even now, when many grown children have moved far away from their families, many of them journey home for this important occasion. One week after réveillon, French Canadians sit down for a lavish turkey dinner, either with family members or with friends, and spend the day visiting as they welcome in the New Year.

A Christmas card from the 1900's depicts Père Noël, the French version of Father Christmas.

Now approaching—

MONTREAL AND

QUEBEC CITY

We arrive in Montreal at the conveniently located Central Station. One of the most wonderful things to do in Montreal during the holidays is to see the city's charming cobblestoned streets decked out in holiday decorations. We decide to take a carriage ride along some of these beautiful streets.

Every Saturday evening in December, Montreal has a fireworks display at the Old Port, along the Saint Lawrence River. The fireworks are choreographed to music.

Urban SPARKLE

After fireworks, we visit the Place des Festivals, a large square devoted to urban entertainment. At this square, Montreal holds Luminotherapie each year, an outdoor show of lighted art pieces created by local designers and architects.

A Song and a PRAYER

Finally we attend Montreal's *Défilé* (day fee lay) du Père Noël, or Santa Claus parade. The parade began in Montreal in 1925 and has been held most years since then. Thousands of children wait to catch their first glimpse of Santa for the season.

A sculpture (right) located at the headquarters of Montreal's world-famous *Cirque du Soleil* (serk duh soh lay). All new touring shows for the company premiere in Montreal, so always check to see what is playing when you visit there.

We arrive by horse-drawn carriage at *Notre-Dame* (noh truh dahm) Basilica of Montreal (bottom). The church gives us a sense of the city's history. The structure in place today (completed in 1830) stands where two smaller chapels dedicated to the Virgin Mary stood before (one completed in 1642, replaced by another completed in 1683). Masses celebrated in the church are in French (left). The basilica is known for its music, and concerts and choir recitals are held here. The church has a magnificent pipe organ (directly below).

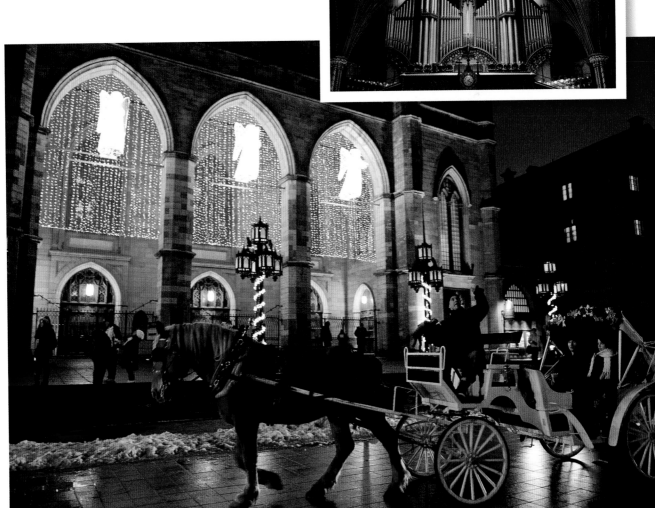

Quebec City

We leave Montreal for Quebec City. After a three-hour train trip, we enter Quebec City's *Gare du Palais* (gahr duh puh LAY, or *palace station*), near Quebec's *Vieux Quebec* (veew kay beck, or *Old Town*).

We take a taxi from the station, and as we round a hill, our hotel comes into view. The Chateau Frontenac (above) is a symbol of Quebec City and one of the most photographed hotels in the world. It sits on a hill overlooking the St. Lawrence River. It is another of the historic hotels originally built in the late 1800's by the Canadian Pacific Railway.

The upper part of Quebec City is surrounded by a stone wall, built centuries ago by first the French and later the British armies as a means of fortification.

On Christmas Eve, we leave the hotel and walk to the nearby Notre-Dame Basilica Cathedral (Our Lady of Quebec City) to attend Mass.

We've timed our stay in Quebec City to allow us to have Christmas dinner the next day at our hotel. The annual dinner-dance in the ballroom of the Chateau Frontenac is a tradition in Quebec City.

Fun & ADVENTURE

The next day, on Dufferin Terrace outside of our hotel, we spend the morning taking a few trips down the toboggan run. The ice-covered ramp is 270 feet (82 meters) long and allows toboggans to reach speeds of up to 60 miles (90 kilometers) per hour before coming to a stop. The ramp, known as *Les Glissades de la Terrace* (lay glee sahd duh lah tehr rass), has been operating for more than a century. At the bottom of the ramp is a small building that sells sweets; you can watch vendors pour hot maple syrup on snow to make a lovely treat.

Later, we visit Quebec City's *Marché du Vieux-Port* (mah shay duh veew pour, or *Old Port Market*), which holds an annual Christmas market. Thousands of local products are available, and gourmets from around the world shop here.

Quebec City abounds in tiny, charming cafes and bistros. Really, events are almost unnecessary in this old-world city. To stroll the lanes and stop at charming eateries is a delight.

We leave beautiful Quebec City and board a train headed for the Maritime Provinces. As we head for Halifax, the end of our tour, our train crosses the province of New Brunswick.

Customs of the Acadians—
Another French–Speaking People

Along New Brunswick's Northumberland Strait, midnight Mass, réveillon, and many other French Christmas traditions light up the season for another group of French-speaking Canadians—the Acadians. In the early 1600's, France established the colony of Acadia in what are now Nova Scotia, southern New Brunswick, and Prince Edward Island. When the British came to govern the land 100 years later, France abandoned the colony and the people who resided there. In 1755, the British burned their settlements and drove the Acadians from their land.

Scattered in exile, the former French settlers yearned to reclaim the Canadian land they now considered home. In a few years, they began to return. Descendants of the original colonists arrived in strength in the late 1800's, settling in eastern New Brunswick, Nova Scotia, and on Prince Edward Island.

Today, after nearly four centuries, the Acadians continue to be a strong cultural force in Canada's Maritime Provinces. They comprise more than 30 percent of the population of New Brunswick, concentrated along the province's eastern coast. With its permanent mix of English- and French-speaking citizens, New Brunswick is today Canada's only officially bilingual province.

Canada's Acadians celebrate their Christmas traditions with pride. To mark the weeks preceding Christmas, Acadians construct Advent wreaths in the shape of a cross, which are placed at the foot of the altars in churches. Four candles adorn each wreath. The candles are lighted in succession on the Sundays leading up to Christmas.

Christmas Eve, with its religious service and réveillon, is in the French tradition. But uniquely Acadian foods highlight the family feast. An Acadian favorite likely to be on any holiday table is *pâté à la râpure* (pah tay ah lah rah poor), or rappie pie. This hearty dish is made of layered potatoes, meat, and onions with plenty of bacon, salt, and pepper.

In Acadian communities, the crèche, or nativity scene, is the dominant Christmas decoration. Inside and outside churches and under the Christmas trees in Acadian homes, the crèche is always present. In place of Santas and snowmen, Acadian families display lighted nativity scenes, often life-sized, on their front lawns at Christmastime.

A print depicts British troops forcing the Acadians from their homes and land.

At Christmastime, some Acadian children prepare for their parents a traditional Acadian Christmas gift, the Bouquet Spirituel. In years past, young Acadian children, under the guidance of the nuns at school, decorated little cards with dried flowers and colorful drawings. On these cards, each child carefully counted up all the prayers he or she said in the weeks leading up to Christmas. Inspired by the special feelings of the season, and maybe by sibling competition, children often presented their parents with cards marked with hundreds of prayers.

When preparing the *gâteau des rois* (gah toh day rwah, or *king's cake*) for the Feast of the Epiphany, Acadian tradition is to bake into the cake a ring and a piece of silver along with the bean and pea. While the bean and pea determine which "king" and "queen" shall reign over the party, the ring reveals the woman who will be first to marry, and the silver marks one who will be rich. When an unexpected person gets the ring or silver, the merriment truly begins.

Customs of a First Nations People

The First Canadians

Long before Christmas came to North America, the deep Canadian woods, with their bounty of balsam, spruce, and cedar trees and snowy drifts, were warmed in the darkest days of winter by celebration.

Not long after Columbus arrived in the New World, legions of European fishermen discovered the teeming fishing waters of the eastern shore of North America and began making annual summer visits across the Atlantic.

A painting depicts hunters and fishermen of the Mi'kmaq (Micmac) tribe in the 1800's. In the early 1500's, the Mi'kmaq traded with French, Portuguese, and Spanish fishing crews who visited Canada. After Jacques Cartier, a French explorer, came to Canada in 1534, the Indians traded their furs for beads and knives.

The European ships became such familiar sights that, in 1534, when explorer Jacques Cartier first entered Chaleur Bay, he was greeted by aboriginal peoples who presented beaver skins to trade. The fur trade expanded rapidly, bringing more and more French trappers and traders. When Champlain founded Quebec City in 1608, permanent contact between the aboriginal peoples of Canada and the Europeans was established. Quick on the heels of Champlain came French Jesuit missionaries. During the late 1600's to the mid-1700's, the Jesuits successfully established a number of Christian villages among the First Nations peoples. With these missionaries, Christmas came to Canada. Many of the aboriginal peoples converted to Christianity soon after encountering the European missionaries. Over time, aboriginal peoples and Europeans intermarried. As cultures blended, even more native peoples adopted the Christian faith.

A Season to Rejoice

For many of Canada's First Nations groups, winter is a traditional season of feasting and celebration. Sharing and gift-giving ceremonies are central to the cultural beliefs of many of Canada's First Nations peoples.

The Mi'kmaq were the first known inhabitants of Nova Scotia. At the Eskasoni Reserve, a devout Christian community of Mi'kmaq peoples has thrived since 1610, when Mi'kmaq chief Membertou was baptized in the faith by a visiting Jesuit priest. Today, Mi'kmaq Christians decorate their homes with spruce boughs, sing holiday hymns in their proudly preserved tribal language, and whisper special prayers each night of Advent. The Mi'kmaq Christmas observance combines First Nations tradition and Christian beliefs in a rich celebration of Christmas. It begins with a processional Mass at the Catholic church on Christmas Eve and ends with a traditional Mi'kmaq dance.

A French Jesuit missionary preaches to First Nations peoples in this hand-colored woodcut from the 1800's.

THE MARITIME PROVINCES

Churches and homes on a bay in Nova Scotia.

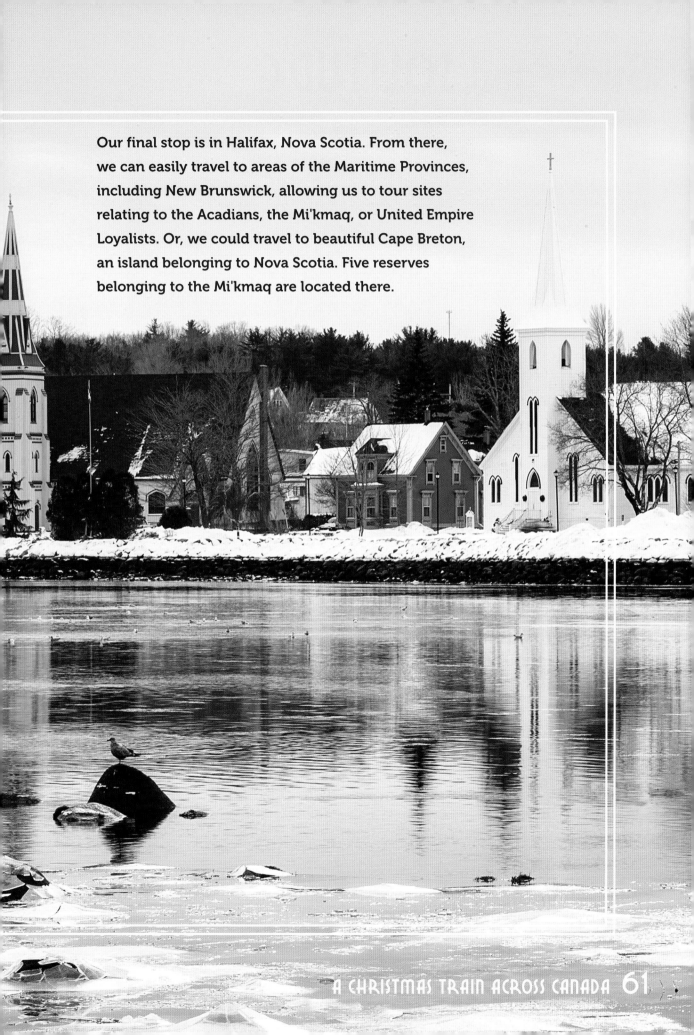

Our final stop is in Halifax, Nova Scotia. From there, we can easily travel to areas of the Maritime Provinces, including New Brunswick, allowing us to tour sites relating to the Acadians, the Mi'kmaq, or United Empire Loyalists. Or, we could travel to beautiful Cape Breton, an island belonging to Nova Scotia. Five reserves belonging to the Mi'kmaq are located there.

Snow and SOLITUDE

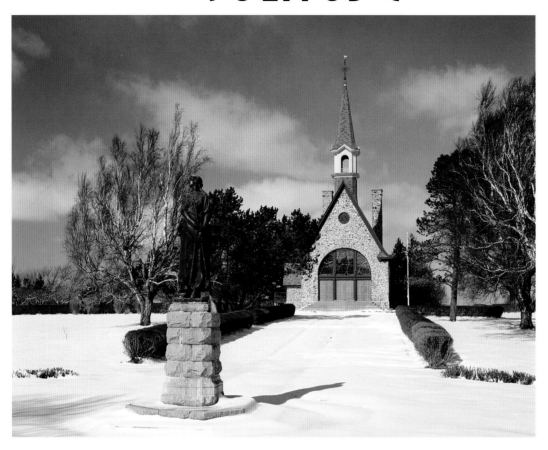

A statue (above), sculpted by Louis-Philippe Hébert, of Evangeline, a character from a poem by American Henry Wadsworth Longfellow that concerns the expulsion of the Acadians from Canada. The statue stands in front of a church in Grand-Pré National Historic Site, Nova Scotia.

A traditional wigwam of the Mi'kmaq people.

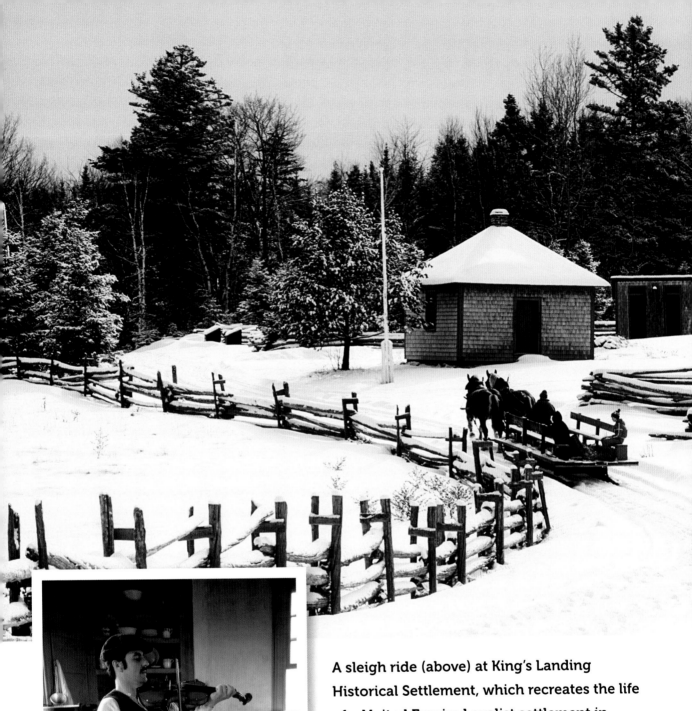

A sleigh ride (above) at King's Landing Historical Settlement, which recreates the life of a United Empire Loyalist settlement in New Brunswick in the 1800's. The Loyalists were Americans who had stood by the British crown during the American Revolutionary War and who fled the United States after the war.

A fiddler (left) at the Acadian Historic Village near Caraquet, New Brunswick.

Christmas CRAFTS

A Christmas Train

All aboard! With some pasta and a hot-glue gun, you can make this charming Christmas train. (When using a hot-glue gun, be careful not to burn yourself. Always ask an adult to do the gluing for you.)

What you will need:

- ruler
- pencil
- sharp knife
- hot-glue gun
- pasta (as shown*)

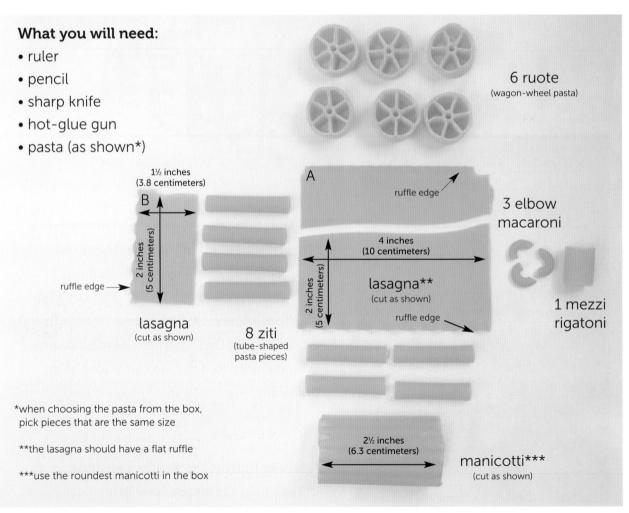

6 ruote
(wagon-wheel pasta)

1½ inches
(3.8 centimeters)

B

2 inches
(5 centimeters)

ruffle edge →

lasagna
(cut as shown)

8 ziti
(tube-shaped
pasta pieces)

A

ruffle edge

4 inches
(10 centimeters)

2 inches
(5 centimeters)

lasagna**
(cut as shown)

ruffle edge

3 elbow
macaroni

1 mezzi
rigatoni

2½ inches
(6.3 centimeters)

manicotti***
(cut as shown)

*when choosing the pasta from the box,
pick pieces that are the same size

**the lasagna should have a flat ruffle

***use the roundest manicotti in the box

Cutting the pasta

With a sharp knife and gentle pressure, use a sawing motion to cut as you keep turning the manicotti. You will be creating a groove in the pasta (right). Because the pasta is hard, this will take some time, but eventually the groove will become deep enough and the pieces will break apart. If you try to cut the pasta from top to bottom in one cut, you risk breaking or cracking it.

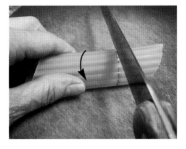
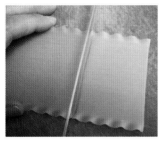

The lasagna noodle is much easier to cut. Again, use a sharp knife and gentle pressure to "saw" through the pasta.

Important: Have an adult complete the cutting step.

The gluing process

Be sure an adult also handles this step. The glue gun and glue are hot and can burn you.

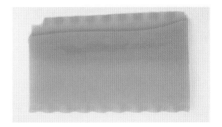

1. Because lasagna noodle A (see left) is too wide, it needs to be cut, but the ruffled edges are needed for both sides. Overlap the two pieces of A to form a rectangle a little more than 2 inches wide with a ruffled edge on both sides.

2. The side shown above will be the floor of the engine. Turn it over and glue the ruote pieces as shown.

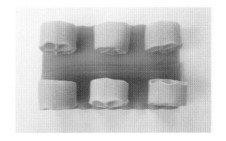

3. Flip the piece over and glue the manicotti in the center, flush with one end of the lasagna noodle.

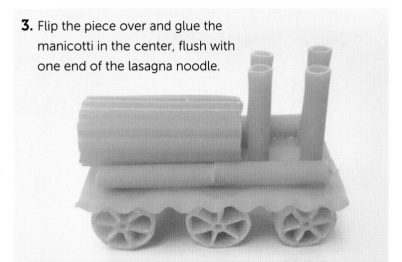

4. On each side of the manicotti, center two ziti pieces on the lasagna and glue. Repeat this step on the other side.

Then glue the remaining four ziti standing up, as shown.

5. To make the smoke stack, glue the elbow macaroni to one end of the mezzi rigatoni, as shown. Glue the other end to the barrel of the engine.

6. Lastly, glue the small lasagna (B) to the top of the standing ziti. The ruffle edge should be at the back of the engine.

Turn the page to see directions for a coal car and a tree.

Note: If you make a mistake while gluing, the pieces can be gently pulled apart if the glue has not fully set. Before you try again, let the glue cool and dry and then peel it off the pasta.

To make the coal car
you will need these pasta pieces

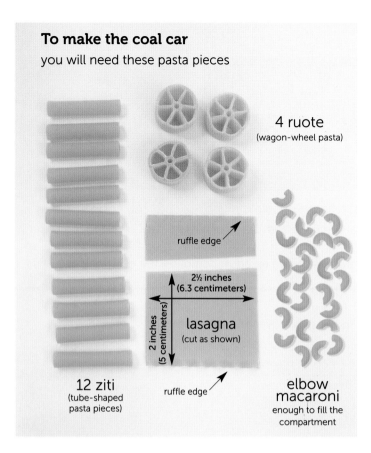

4 ruote
(wagon-wheel pasta)

ruffle edge

2½ inches
(6.3 centimeters)

2 inches
(5 centimeters)

lasagna
(cut as shown)

12 ziti
(tube-shaped
pasta pieces)

ruffle edge

elbow
macaroni
enough to fill the
compartment

7. Repeat steps 1 and 2 shown on page 65 to make the floor and attach the wheels of the coal car.

8. Turn over and glue one ziti on each outside edge of the floor.

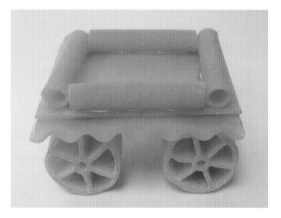

9. Glue two more rows of ziti on top of the first row.

10. Fill the coal car with loose elbow macaroni.

To make the tree
you will need
these pasta pieces

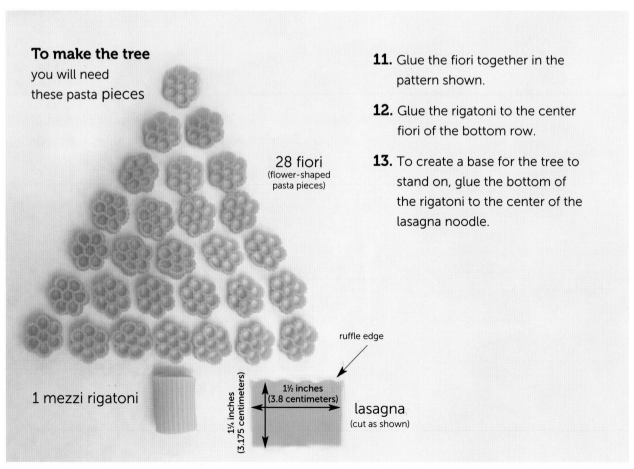

28 fiori
(flower-shaped
pasta pieces)

1 mezzi rigatoni

ruffle edge

1¼ inches
(3.175 centimeters)

1½ inches
(3.8 centimeters)

lasagna
(cut as shown)

11. Glue the fiori together in the pattern shown.

12. Glue the rigatoni to the center fiori of the bottom row.

13. To create a base for the tree to stand on, glue the bottom of the rigatoni to the center of the lasagna noodle.

A Merry Chris-moose

Let a moose loose! (Our Christmas moose, in fact, which is easy to make.) A bow or wreath completes this Christmas craft.

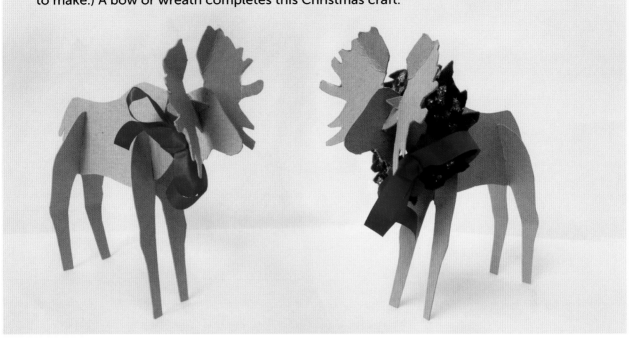

What you will need:

- tracing paper
- pencil
- brown craftboard, sturdy enough to stand but lightweight enough to cut with a scissors
- scissors
- green felt
- glue
- silvery-white glitter
- red ribbon

1. Using tracing paper, copy the patterns on page 68 and cut them out of the craftboard. Be sure to cut the slots as well.

2. Make a fold in the antlers and hind legs where indicated by the dashed lines.

3. Assemble the moose by sliding the pieces into the slots as shown.

4. Finish off your moose by tying a ribbon or hanging a wreath around its neck. (To make the wreath, see page 68.)

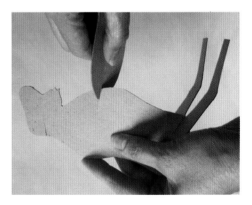

To make the wreath

5. Cut a 2¾ inch (7 centimeters) open circle out of the craftboard.

6. Cut elliptical leaf shapes out of the felt. You can use this pattern at right. Leaves do not have to be perfect. You will need between 68 and 80 leaves, depending on how they fit on the circle.

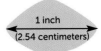

1 inch
(2.54 centimeters)

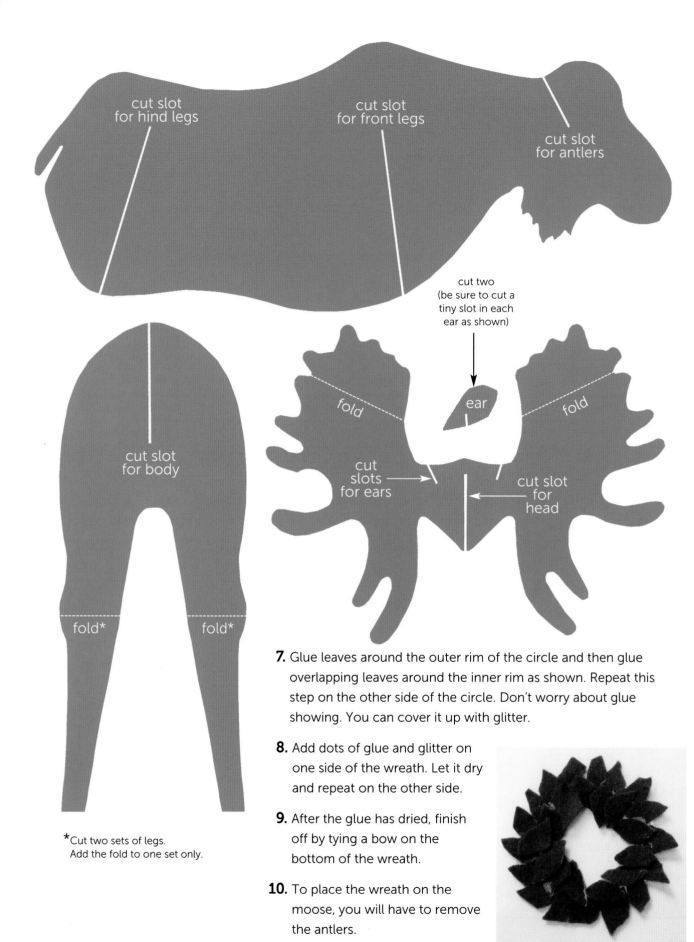

cut slot
for hind legs

cut slot
for front legs

cut slot
for antlers

cut two
(be sure to cut a
tiny slot in each
ear as shown)

fold

ear

fold

cut slot
for body

cut
slots
for ears

cut slot
for
head

fold*

fold*

*Cut two sets of legs.
Add the fold to one set only.

7. Glue leaves around the outer rim of the circle and then glue overlapping leaves around the inner rim as shown. Repeat this step on the other side of the circle. Don't worry about glue showing. You can cover it up with glitter.

8. Add dots of glue and glitter on one side of the wreath. Let it dry and repeat on the other side.

9. After the glue has dried, finish off by tying a bow on the bottom of the wreath.

10. To place the wreath on the moose, you will have to remove the antlers.

Maple Leaf Mitten

This mitten ornament displays the national symbol of Canada.

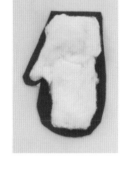

What you will need:

- tracing paper
- pencil
- red and white felt
- scissors
- 2 cotton balls
- white yarn and needle with a large eye
- white thread and needle
- glue

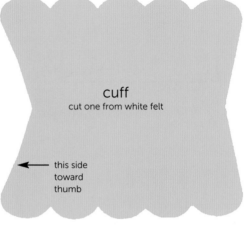

cuff
cut one from white felt

← this side toward thumb

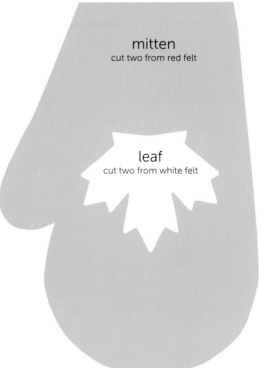

mitten
cut two from red felt

leaf
cut two from white felt

1. Using tracing paper, copy the patterns and cut them out of the felt.

2. Spread the cotton balls apart to cover one piece of felt as shown.

3. Place the other piece of felt on top and stitch the two pieces together with the white yarn.

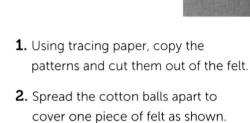

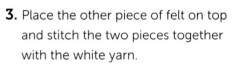

4. Make a hanger by threading yarn through the mitten, the cuff, and then back out again. Complete with a knot.

5. Slide the cuff down to the edge of the mitten. Using thread, sew the sides of the cuff together and attach to the mitten.

6. Glue one maple leaf to each side of the mitten.

Christmas RECIPES

Oyster Soup

3 tbsp. butter, melted
1 tsp. finely chopped onion
1½ pints of oysters with liquid
1½ cups milk
½ cup heavy cream

salt to taste
white pepper to taste
2 egg yolks, beaten
2 tbsp. chopped
  fresh parsley

In the top pan of a double boiler, melt butter over direct heat. Sauté onion in butter until onion is transparent. Add oysters with liquid, milk, cream, salt, and pepper. Place pan over boiling water in the bottom pan of the double boiler. When the milk becomes hot and the oysters float, remove from heat. In a small bowl, gradually add 2 or 3 tablespoons of hot soup to beaten yolks. After mixing, slowly add eggs to the hot soup. Heat slowly for another minute or so, but do not allow to boil. Garnish with parsley and serve immediately.

Makes 4 servings.

Meat Ball Stew

(Ragout de Boulettes)

1 medium onion
1 clove garlic, minced
2 tbsp. butter, melted
1 lb. ground pork
1 tsp. ground ginger

1 tsp. ground cloves
2 tbsp. olive oil
3 cups beef stock
1 tbsp. flour

Sauté onion and garlic in butter until onion is transparent. In a medium bowl, mix together pork, ginger, cloves, and onion-and-garlic mixture. Shape meat into 2-inch balls. In a large skillet, brown meat balls in olive oil over medium heat.

Add beef stock and simmer 30 minutes. Blend flour with a small amount of water. Add flour mixture to beef stock, stirring constantly until sauce thickens.

Makes 8 servings.

Mincemeat

(Note: Make this recipe two weeks before you plan to use the mincemeat.)

4 cups finely chopped
    peeled apples
4 cups raisins
½ cup citron, chopped

2 tsp. cinnamon
¼ tsp. ground cloves
1 tsp. nutmeg
¼ tsp. salt

3 cups brown sugar
3 lemons, grated rind and juice
1 cup apple juice
¼ cup brandy (optional)

In a large saucepan, combine apples, raisins, citron, spices, salt, brown sugar, the juice and grated rinds of the lemons, and apple juice. Bring to a boil. Reduce heat and simmer 1½ hours, stirring frequently.

Remove mixture from heat; add brandy, if desired. Spoon into hot, sterilized canning jars. Process in boiling-water bath for 15 minutes. Mincemeat will be ready for use in about 2 weeks.

Makes about 7 cups.

For Mincemeat Pie: Preheat oven to 425 °F.
For each double-crust, 9-inch pie (below), mix two cups mincemeat with 2 cups chopped apple. Spoon into prepared pie shell; top with pastry and seal edges. Prick top crust with fork to vent. Bake for 15 minutes; reduce heat to 350 °F and bake for 30 minutes more or until pastry is lightly browned.

Pastry for 9-Inch Double-Crust Pie
(for Cipaillle, Tourtiere, or Mincemeat Pie)

2½ cups flour
dash salt

½ cup butter
½ cup shortening

6-8 tbsp. water

In a large mixing bowl, combine flour and salt. Cut in butter and shortening using a pastry knife until the largest pieces of the mixture are about the size of a pea. Sprinkle water over the mixture, one tablespoon at a time. Use a fork to gently distribute the water until a soft dough forms. Gather the dough into a ball. Separate into two equal balls. Refrigerate for about an hour.

Remove one ball of dough from refrigerator and place on a lightly floured surface. Press ball with palm of hand to flatten slightly. With floured rolling pin, roll from center to edges until crust is ⅛-inch thick. Repeat process with the other ball.

Makes dough for one double-crust 9-inch pie.

Cipaille (see pye, or *Meat and Potato Pie*)

2 lbs. boneless,
   skinless chicken breast
2 lbs. beef tenderloin
2 lbs. pork tenderloin
2 large onions, chopped
2 large potatoes,
   peeled, cut into 1-inch cubes
½ tsp. salt

pepper to taste
¼ tsp. nutmeg
¼ tsp. cinnamon
¼ tsp. allspice
2 cups chicken or beef stock
double batch of pie pastry,
   see recipe page 71

Make enough pastry for two 9-inch double-crust pies, using the recipe on page 71.

Cut chicken and meats into 1-inch cubes; place in a large bowl. Mix in onions. Cover and refrigerate overnight.

Preheat oven to 400 °F. In a small bowl, combine spices. Spray the bottom and sides of a 3-quart casserole dish with cooking spray. Divide pastry dough into four equal parts. Roll out each to ¼-inch thickness, large enough to line the bottom of the casserole. Line casserole dish with one pastry round. Spoon in one-third of the meat mixture, one-third of the potatoes, and one-third of the spices. Place another pastry round on top of the potatoes. Prick pastry with a fork to allow steam to vent. Top pastry with another third of the meat mixture, potatoes, and spices, and another pastry round. Again, prick the pastry with a fork. Repeat layering once more, finishing with pastry. Cut a 1-inch slit in the center of the top pastry.

Pour enough stock through the slit until liquid appears at the side of the dish. Cover casserole dish and bake 45 minutes. Reduce oven temperature to 250 °F and continue baking for 6 hours or until top crust is golden-brown.

Makes 8 servings.

Candied Cranberries

2½ cups sugar   1½ cups water   1 quart cranberries

In a saucepan, boil water and place a steamer inside pan. In another saucepan, stir sugar in water over medium-high heat. Bring mixture to a boil, stirring constantly. Pour the boiling mixture over the cranberries in a large heat-resistant bowl. Place bowl in steamer for 45 minutes. Remove bowl and cool cranberries without stirring. Set in a warm, dry place for 3 to 4 days. When the syrup has a jellylike consistency, remove cranberries and allow to dry 3 days longer. Turn cranberries often so they will dry completely. When they can be handled easily, store in a tightly covered container.

Makes about 1 quart.

English Steamed Plum Pudding

½ cup presifted flour
½ cup raisins
½ lb. suet, chopped
½ lb. dried currants
½ lb. citron, chopped

1½ tsp. nutmeg
1½ tsp. cinnamon
1 tsp mace
dash salt
¼ cup brown sugar

4 eggs, separated
3 tbsp. cream
¼ cup brandy
1½ cups breadcrumbs
hard sauce, see below

Sprinkle some of the flour on the raisins, suet, currants, and citron. Sift the remaining flour with nutmeg, cinnamon, mace, salt, and brown sugar. Combine the raisin mixture with the sifted ingredients. Add egg yolks, cream, brandy, and breadcrumbs. Whip egg whites until stiff. Gently fold egg whites into raisin mixture. Pour pudding into a greased ½-gallon (2-quart) pudding mold. (Hint: Line mold with cheesecloth for easy removal.) Place mold in a large pot filled with water that reaches halfway up the mold. Cover mold; steam 6 hours. Store covered in a cool place for several weeks before serving. If desired, serve with hard sauce.

Hard Sauce

(for English Steamed Plum Pudding)

1 cup sifted powdered
 sugar
½ cup butter

1 tbsp. brandy or rum
dash salt

In a mixing bowl, cream butter and sugar. Beat until well blended and fluffy. Slowly add brandy and salt. When sauce is smooth, chill thoroughly.

Canadian Doughnuts

3 cups flour
¾ cup sugar
3 tsp. baking powder
1 tsp. baking soda
½ tsp. nutmeg

½ tsp. cinnamon
¼ tsp. salt
½ cup buttermilk
3 tbsp. butter, melted
2 eggs, slightly beaten

vegetable oil for frying
cinnamon-sugar mixture
 (1 part cinnamon to
 4 parts sugar)
powdered sugar

Mix together flour, sugar, baking powder, baking soda, nutmeg, cinnamon, and salt; set aside. Blend buttermilk and butter into eggs; gradually add dry ingredients to make a soft dough. Chill in refrigerator 2 to 3 hours.

On a floured board, roll dough to ¼-inch thickness. Using a floured doughnut cutter, cut out doughnuts. Cook in hot oil for 1 to 2 minutes per side or until golden brown. Drain on paper towels. Roll warm doughnuts in a cinnamon-sugar mixture or powdered sugar, if desired.

Makes about 1 ½ dozen doughnuts.

Sugar Pie

pastry for 9-inch
  single-crust pie (below)
1½ cups brown sugar

¾ cup whipping cream
8 tsp. cornstarch

Preheat oven to 425 °F. Line pie pan with pastry. In a medium bowl, mix together brown sugar, whipping cream, and cornstarch. Pour mixture into prepared pie shell. Bake 10 minutes, then lower temperature to 325 °F and continue baking for 30 minutes or until filling is set and golden.

Makes 6 servings.

Maple Syrup Pie

Pastry for 9-inch single-crust pie (below)

¼ cup flour
½ cup water

1 cup maple syrup
1 egg, slightly beaten

2 tbsp. butter
whipped cream

Preheat oven to 450 °F. Line 9-inch pie pan with pastry; prick several times with a fork. Bake pie shell for 10 minutes or until lightly browned. Allow pie shell to cool.

Mix flour and water until smooth. In a medium saucepan, stir together flour mixture and maple syrup. Stir in egg. Cook over medium heat, stirring constantly until thick. Add butter and stir until melted.

Pour mixture into cooled pie shell. Allow pie to cook at room temperature until set. Serve topped with whipped cream.

Makes 8 servings.

Pastry for 9-inch Single-Crust Pie

(for Sugar Pie or Maple Syrup Pie)

1½ cups sifted all-purpose flour
½ tsp. salt

½ cup butter
4 to 5 tbsp. very cold water

Sift flour and salt into a medium mixing bowl. Using a pastry knife, cut in butter until pieces are the size of small peas. Sprinkle 1 tbsp. water over the contents of bowl; toss gently with fork to mix. Repeat this step until all water has been added. Form mixture into a ball; place on lightly floured surface. Press ball with palm of hand to flatten slightly. With floured rolling pin, roll from center to edges until crust is ⅛-inch thick.

Mulled Cider

1 quart apple cider 4 or 5 whole cloves cinnamon stick

In a medium saucepan, mix together ingredients over medium heat; heat well, but do not allow to boil. Strain out the spices before serving.

Makes 4 servings.

Honey Cake

1 cup honey	3 cups flour	¼ tsp. salt
½ cup butter	1½ tsp. baking soda	½ cup cooled
1 cup brown sugar	1 tsp. baking powder	strong coffee
4 eggs, separated	½ tsp. cinnamon	½ cup walnuts,
1 tsp. vanilla	½ tsp. ground ginger	chopped

Preheat oven to 325 °F. In a small saucepan, bring honey to a boil; allow to cool to room temperature. In a large bowl, cream butter and brown sugar. Beat in egg yolks, one at a time. Add cooled honey and vanilla.

In a separate bowl, sift together flour, baking soda, baking powder, cinnamon, ginger, and salt. Alternate blending coffee and dry ingredients into butter mixture.

Stir in nuts. Beat egg whites until stiff but not dry; fold into batter. Pour batter into a well-greased loaf pan. Bake for 1 hour. Cool on rack 10 minutes. Remove from pan. Once cooled, wrap in plastic wrap to keep moist. Stored in a cool place, this cake will improve with age.

Makes 10 to 12 servings.

Scottish Shortbread

1 cup butter
½ cup sugar, white or brown
2 cups flour

Preheat oven to 275 °F. Cream butter and sugar. Gradually mix in flour. Knead dough until smooth. On lightly floured surface, roll dough into ½-inch-thick round. Place on an ungreased cookie sheet; prick with a fork and crimp edges. Bake 1 hour or until light brown. Cut into wedges while still warm.

Makes 12 wedges

Christmas CAROLS

'Twas in the Moon of Wintertime

English translation: J.E. Middleton
Andante

Original words in Huron Indian
By Father Jean de Brebeuf, 1593-1649

Lyrics:
1. 'Twas in the moon of win-ter-time when all the birds had fled, That might-y Git-chi Man-i-tou sent an-gel choirs in-stead. Be-fore their light the

stars grew dim, And wan - d'ring hun - ters heard the hymn: ——

Refrain

"Je - sus, your King, is born. Je - sus is born. *In ex - cel - sis glo - ri - a!"*

2. Within a lodge of broken bark
   the tender Babe was found,
   A ragged robe of rabbit skin
   enwrapped His beauty round.
   And as the hunter braves
   drew nigh,
   The angel song rang loud
   and high——
   "Jesus, your king, is born, Jesus is
   born. *In excelsis gloria!"*

3. The earliest moon of wintertime
   is not so round and fair,
   As was the ring of glory on the
   helpless infant there.
   While Chiefs from far before
   him knelt,
   With gifts of fox and beaver
   pelt.——
   "Jesus, your king, is born. Jesus is
   born. *In excelsis gloria!"*

4. O children of the forest free,
   O sons of Manitou,
   The Holy Child of earth and
   Heav'n is born today for you.
   Come, kneel before the
   radiant Boy
   Who brings you beauty, peace
   and joy.——
   "Jesus, your king, is born. Jesus is
   born. *In excelsis gloria!"*

Whence Art Thou, My Maiden?

D'où Viens-Tu, Bergère?

Translation: William McLennan, 1886

Traditional French Canadian

1. "Whence art thou, my mai - den, whence art thou?"
1. *"D'où viens - tu, ber - gè - re, d'où viens - tu?"*

"I come from the sta - ble where, this ver - y night,_____
"Je viens de l'é - tab - le, de m'y pro - me - ner,_____

I, a shep—herd maid — en, saw a won — drous__sight."
J'ai vu un mi — ra — cle ce soir ar — ri — vé."

2. "What saw'st thou, my maiden,
   what saw'st thou?
   What saw'st thou, my maiden,
   what saw'st thou?"
   "There within a manger,
   a little Child I saw
   Lying, softly sleeping,
   on a bed of straw."

3. "Nothing more, my maiden,
   nothing more?
   Nothing more, my maiden,
   nothing more?"
   "There I saw the mother
   her sweet Baby hold,
   And the father, Joseph,
   trembling with the cold."

4. "Nothing more, my maiden,
   nothing more?
   Nothing more, my maiden,
   nothing more?"
   "I saw ass and oxen,
   kneeling meek and mild,
   With their gentle breathing
   warm the holy Child."

5. "Nothing more, my maiden,
   nothing more?
   Nothing more, my maiden,
   nothing more?"
   "There were three bright angels
   come down from the sky,
   Singing forth sweet praises
   to our God on high."

2. *"Qu'as-tu vu, bergère,*
   qu'as-tu vu?
   "Qu'as-tu vu, bergère,
   qu'as-tu vu?"
   "J'ai vu dans la crèche
   un petit enfant
   Sur la paille fraîche,
   mis bien tendrement."

3. *"Rien de plus, bergère,*
   rien de plus?
   Rien de plus, bergère,
   rien de plus?"
   "Saint' Marie, sa mère,
   qui lui fait boir' du lait,
   Saint Joseph, son père,
   qui tremble de froid."

4. *"Rien de plus, bergère,*
   rien de plus?
   Rien de plus, bergère,
   rien de plus?"
   "Y-a boeuf et l'âne,
   qui sont par devant
   Avec leur halei
   ne rechauffant l'enfant."

5. *Rien de plus, bergère,*
   rien de plus?
   Rien de plus, bergère,
   rien de plus?"
   "Y-a trois petits anges
   descendus du ciel,
   Chantant les louanges
   du Père éternel."

**Stained glass ceiling window at the
Montreal Notre-Dame Basilica.**

ACKNOWLEDGMENTS

The publishers gratefully acknowledge the following sources for photography. All illustrations and maps were prepared by WORLD BOOK unless otherwise noted.

2-3   © Robert McGouey/Alamy Images

4-5   © Shutterstock

6-7   © Shutterstock; © Fairmont Hotels

8-9   © Alamy Images

10-11   © Hulton Archive/Getty Images; © V&A/Alamy Images

12-13   Twelfth Night Revels in the Great Hall (1838) Lithograph by Joseph Nash, The Stapleton Collection (© Bridgeman Art Library)

14-15   © Shutterstock; © Gunter Marx, Alamy Images

16-17   © Michael Wheatley, Alamy Images; © All Canada Photos/Alamy Images; © Cameron Spencer, Getty Images

18-19   © Courtesy of Capilano Suspension Bridge Park

20-21   © Fairmont Hotels; © Xinhua/Alamy Images; © Michael Wheatley, Alamy Images

22-23   © All Canada Photos/Alamy Images

24-25   © Fairmont Hotels

26-27   © Fairmont Hotels; © Stephen Giardina, Alamy Images

28-29   © Shutterstock; © Thinkstock

30-31   © Michael Interisano, AGE Fotostock; © Dave Pattinson, Alamy Images © Calgary Zoo; © Svetlana Yanova

32-33   © Shutterstock

34-35   © Shutterstock; © Peter Mintz, Alamy Images

36-37   © Shutterstock

38-39   © Mark Bergman; © Shutterstock; © Richard Lautens, Toronto Star/Getty Images; © Shutterstock

40-43   © Chronicle/Alamy Images

44-45   © Bridgeman Art Library

46-47   © Shutterstock; © Thinkstock

48-49   © Cindy Boyce, Quartier des spectacles

50-51   © Andrew Soong, Xinhua/Alamy Images; © Ros Drinkwater, Alamy Images; © Mia & Klaus Matthes, SuperStock; © Shutterstock; © David Coleman, Alamy Images

52-53   © Thinkstock; © Shutterstock; © Fairmont Hotels

54-55   © Thinkstock; © Yvette Cardozo, Alamy Images; © Jeremy Graham, dbimages/Alamy Images; © Robert Chiasson, All Canada Photos/SuperStock

56-57   © North Wind Picture Archives/Alamy Images

58-59   © DeAgostini/SuperStock; © North Wind Picture Archives/Alamy Images

60-61   © All Canada Photos/Alamy Images

62-63   © Gary Neil Corbett, SuperStock; © iStock photo; © Bill Brooks, Alamy Images

64-69   © Brenda Tropinski, WORLD BOOK Photo

70-80   © Shutterstock